CHAPTER 1 - LIMITS

1.1 - Evaluating Limits

A **limit** is simply a value a function *approaches* (let's denote this value c) as it gets closer and closer to a specific value (let's denote this value a) from both sides.

$$\lim_{x \to a} f(x) = c$$

However, the function may not necessarily equal c at a, or might not even exist at a, depending on whether it has a discontinuity (discussed in Section 1.2) or not.

$$f(a) \overset{?}{=} c$$

If the function does indeed satisfy $f(a) = c$ (no discontinuity), then you can just plug a into function f and get the value of the limit.

$$\lim_{x \to a} f(x) = f(a) = c$$

EXAMPLE 1.1.1:

Evaluate $\lim_{x \to 2} x^2$.

$$\lim_{x \to 2} x^2 = (2)^2 = \boxed{4}$$

Some mildly important limit rules:

$$\lim_{x \to a} [k \cdot f(x)] = k \lim_{x \to a} [f(x)]$$

$$\lim_{x \to a} [f(x) + g(x)] = \lim_{x \to a} [f(x)] + \lim_{x \to a} [g(x)]$$

$$\lim_{x \to a} [f(x) \cdot g(x)] = \left(\lim_{x \to a} [f(x)] \right) \left(\lim_{x \to a} [g(x)] \right)$$

$$\lim_{x \to a} \left[\frac{f(x)}{g(x)} \right] = \frac{\lim_{x \to a} [f(x)]}{\lim_{x \to a} [g(x)]}$$

If substituting gives an **indeterminate form** (simply substituting x in gives an answer of $0/0$ or ∞/∞), you can try a few methods to evaluate the limit.

Factoring.

EXAMPLE 1.1.2:

Evaluate $\lim\limits_{x \to -3} \frac{x^2+x-6}{x^2-9}$.

$$\lim\limits_{x \to -3} \frac{x^2+x-6}{x^2-9} = \lim\limits_{x \to -3} \frac{(x+3)(x-2)}{(x+3)(x-3)} = \lim\limits_{x \to -3} \frac{x-2}{x-3} = \boxed{\frac{5}{6}}$$

Multiplying by the Conjugate.

EXAMPLE 1.1.3:

Evaluate $\lim\limits_{x \to 0} \frac{\sqrt{x+5}-\sqrt{5}}{x}$.

$$\lim\limits_{x \to 0} \frac{\sqrt{x+5}-\sqrt{5}}{x} = \lim\limits_{x \to 0} \frac{\left(\sqrt{x+5}-\sqrt{5}\right)\left(\sqrt{x+5}+\sqrt{5}\right)}{x\left(\sqrt{x+5}+\sqrt{5}\right)} = \lim\limits_{x \to 0} \frac{x+5-5}{x\left(\sqrt{x+5}+\sqrt{5}\right)} =$$

$$\lim\limits_{x \to 0} \frac{x}{x\left(\sqrt{x+5}+\sqrt{5}\right)} = \lim\limits_{x \to 0} \frac{1}{\sqrt{x+5}+\sqrt{5}} = \boxed{\frac{\sqrt{5}}{10}}$$

Simplifying Fractions.

EXAMPLE 1.1.4:

Evaluate $\lim\limits_{x \to 0} \frac{\frac{1}{3+x}-\frac{1}{3}}{x}$.

$$\lim\limits_{x \to 0} \frac{\frac{1}{3+x}-\frac{1}{3}}{x} = \lim\limits_{x \to 0} \frac{\frac{3-(3+x)}{3x+9}}{x} = \lim\limits_{x \to 0} \frac{-x}{x(3x+9)} = \lim\limits_{x \to 0} -\frac{1}{(3x+9)} = \boxed{-\frac{1}{9}}$$

And so on.

Now for the **Squeeze Theorem**:
If $h(x) \leq f(x) \leq g(x)$ in an interval containing c, and if

$$\lim\limits_{x \to c} h(x) = L = \lim\limits_{x \to c} g(x), \text{ then } \lim\limits_{x \to c} f(x) \text{ exists and is equal to } L.$$

Basically, if two functions share a limit at c, then a third function sandwiched between the two also has the same limit at c. Two very useful limits can be derived from the Squeeze Theorem.

$$\lim\limits_{x \to 0} \frac{\sin(x)}{x} = 1 \text{ and } \lim\limits_{x \to 0} \frac{1-\cos(x)}{x} = 0$$

EXAMPLE 1.1.5:

Evaluate $\lim\limits_{x \to 0} \frac{1-\cos^2(x)}{x}$.

$$\lim_{x \to 0} \frac{1-\cos^2(x)}{x} = \lim_{x \to 0} \frac{(1-\cos(x))(1+\cos(x))}{x}$$

$$\left(\lim_{x \to 0} \frac{1-\cos(x)}{x}\right)\left(\lim_{x \to 0}(1+\cos(x))\right) = (0)\left(\lim_{x \to 0}(1+\cos(x))\right) = \boxed{0}$$

1.2 - Continuity and One-Sided Limits

A function can approach two different values depending on which side it approaches c from.

$$f(x) = \lfloor x \rfloor$$

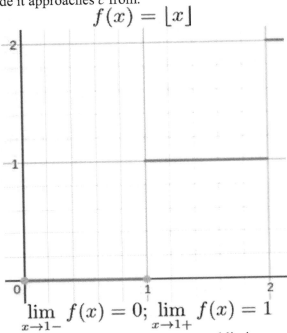

$$\lim_{x \to 1-} f(x) = 0; \lim_{x \to 1+} f(x) = 1$$

These are **one-sided limits**. It's like a normal limit, except you're only approaching it from one side.

We can say that
$$\lim_{x \to a} f(x) \text{ exists and is equal to } c \text{ if and only if}$$

$$\lim_{x \to a-} f(x) = \lim_{x \to a+} f(x) = c.$$

If the two one-sided limits are equal, then the regular limit exists.

Now we discuss continuity. **Continuity** for a function f at $x = c$ simply means that the graph of f is unbroken at f. There are three ways continuity can be broken at $x = c$:

1. The function is not defined at $x = c$ (c is not in the domain of f), for example, an asymptote.

6

2. The limit as x approaches c does not exist (the left and right limits don't equal each other). This is a jump discontinuity.
3. The limit as x approaches c exists, but it isn't equal to f (c). This is a jump discontinuity.

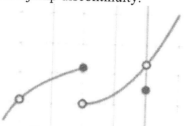

Three discontinuities.

Generally, there are **removable** discontinuities and **nonremovable** discontinuities. Think of removable discontinuities as just removing a point from the function (1 and 3) while a nonremovable discontinuity as just a jump (2).

Furthermore, we can look at continuity on an interval. When we look at just the interval, we disregard anything outside of it.

EXAMPLE 1.2.1:

Is $\frac{1}{x-1}$ continuous over $(2, 4)$?

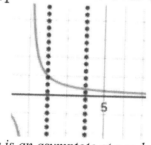

Yes; although there is an asymptote at $x = 1$, the interval we look at is only over $2 < x < 4$.

And finally, we have an important theorem that concerns continuous functions, the **Intermediate Value Theorem,** or just IVT. IVT states that:

If function f is continuous over the closed interval $[a, b]$ and $f(a) < k < f(b)$ for some k, then there is at least one number c such that $f(c) = k$.

Basically, a continuous function passes through every single y-value between its endpoints. It might seem obvious, but it has to be stated directly.

EXAMPLE 1.2.2:

Use IVT to show that the function $f(x) = x^3 + 2x - 1$ has a zero somewhere on the interval $[0, 1]$.

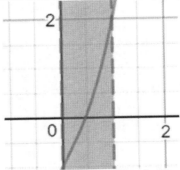

Note that f(x) is continuous over [0, 1]. We can apply IVT:

$$f(0) = 0^3 + 2(0) - 1 = -1$$
$$f(1) = 1^3 + 2(1) - 1 = 2$$

Since f(x) is continuous over [0, 1] and f(0) < 0 < f(1), through IVT there must be a number c in the interval [0, 1] such that f(c) = 0.

Realize that IVT doesn't tell us what number exactly c is; it only tells us that some c exists in this interval. So if you're trying to find the exact value of c, well, IVT can't really help you there.

The Intermediate Value Theorem is one of the four big theorems that we'll discuss, alongside EVT, RT, and MVT (which you'll see later). Make sure to remember all of them as we go along!

1.3 - Infinite Limits and Oscillating Limits

Infinite limits are all about vertical asymptotes - when a function goes up or down infinitely. It's pretty simple. *Note: Technically, limits don't exist when the function goes to infinity; the infinity signs only represent the behavior of the function.*

function goes up	*function goes down*	*function goes both up and down*
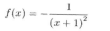		
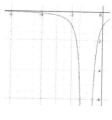	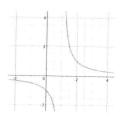	

$$\lim_{x \to 1} f(x) = \infty \qquad \lim_{x \to -1} f(x) = -\infty \qquad \lim_{x \to 1} f(x) = \text{DNE}$$

We can also use one-sided limits to determine the behavior of functions that don't go in only one direction at an asymptote.

$$\lim_{x \to 1-} f(x) = -\infty; \ \lim_{x \to 1+} f(x) = \infty \qquad \lim_{x \to 1-} f(x) = \infty; \ \lim_{x \to 1+} f(x) = -\infty$$

Finally, we get to these weird functions that **oscillate**. What does oscillating mean? Well, as they approach a value, the function bounces back and forth forever. Take the function

$$f(x) = \sin\left(\tfrac{1}{x}\right)$$

for example.

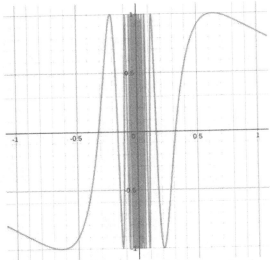

You can see that as $f(x)$ approaches 0, it moves back and forth between -1 and 1. Note that

$$\sin\left(\frac{1}{\frac{2}{\pi}}\right) = 1$$

$$\sin\left(\frac{1}{\frac{2}{3\pi}}\right) = -1$$

$$\sin\left(\frac{1}{\frac{2}{5\pi}}\right) = 1$$

and so on.

Since the function does not converge to a single value, we can say that

$$\lim_{x \to 0} \sin\left(\frac{1}{x}\right) = \text{DNE}$$

This is the general trend for any oscillating function.

10

1.4 - Epsilon-Delta Proofs

Oh, the epsilon-delta proof. It's the formal proof for the existence of a limit, but it's confusing. I'll try to make it as simple as possible, though.

The ε-δ Definition of a Limit:

To prove that

$$\lim_{x \to a} f(x) = L,$$

given an ε, we must find a δ such that

$$0 < |x - a| < \delta \text{ implies } |f(x) - L| < \epsilon.$$

If that can be found, then the limit does indeed exist at L.

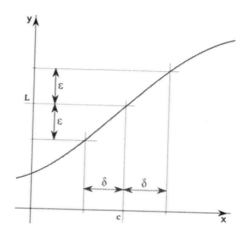

A graphical representation of the ε-δ definition of a limit.

We can do this given a specific value of ε, or just for an arbitrarily small ε. There's more than one method that works when solving these types of equations, too; I've tried to include them all.

Note: there's lots of equations ahead. I suggest you get some pencil and paper and follow along. It helps if you do some of the algebra yourself.

EXAMPLE 1.2.1:

Prove that $\lim_{x \to 2} x^2 - 3 = 1$, for $\epsilon = 0.01$.

$$|(x^2 - 3) - 1| \quad < 0.01$$

$$-0.01 < x^2 - 4 < 0.01$$

$$3.99 < x^2 < 4.01$$

$$1.997 < x < 2.002$$

$$-0.003 < x - 2 < 0.002$$

$$\boxed{\delta = 0.002}$$

Plugging the δ back in:

$$|(x^2 - 3) - 1|$$

$$|x - 2||x + 2| < (0.002)(4.002)$$

$$< 0.008004 < 0.01$$

Note: Since this concerns x around 2, I just add 4 to δ to evaluate $|x + 2|$, because x - 2 is close to zero. You have to be careful with absolute values, though!

EXAMPLE 1.2.2:

Prove that $\lim_{x \to 2} x^2 - 2x = 0$ for an arbitrarily small ϵ.

$$|x^2 - 2x| < \epsilon$$

$$|x||x - 2| < \epsilon$$

We now restrict x near 5; $|x - 2| < 1$. (1 is arbitrary.)
This implies that $-1 < x - 2 < 1 \implies 1 < x < 3$.

So, we should set $\delta = \dfrac{\epsilon}{3}$ because $x < 3$.

Now, for the proof:

$$|x^2 - 2x|$$

$$|x||x - 2| < (3)|x - 2| \text{ (since } x<3)$$

$$< (3)\left(\frac{\epsilon}{3}\right) \text{ (since } |x-2|<\delta=\frac{\epsilon}{3})$$

$$< \epsilon$$

Since this value of δ works, the limit is indeed at 0.

EXAMPLE 1.2.3:

A proof of failure.

Suppose $\lim\limits_{x \to 2} 2x - 3 = 5$. (It doesn't really.)

$$|(2x - 3) - 5| < \epsilon$$

$$-\epsilon < 2x - 8 < \epsilon$$

$$-\epsilon + 8 < 2x < \epsilon + 8$$

$$\frac{-\epsilon + 8}{2} < x < \frac{\epsilon + 8}{2}$$

$$\frac{-\epsilon + 8}{2} - 2 < x - 2 < \frac{\epsilon + 8}{2} - 2$$

$$-\frac{\epsilon + 4}{2} < \frac{-\epsilon + 4}{2} < x - 2 < \frac{\epsilon + 4}{2}$$

$$\delta = \frac{\epsilon + 4}{2}$$

Take note that the bounds of x aren't around x = 2! This already tells us that this limit can't exist, but I'll keep solving through to show through another method that this limit isn't 5.

$$|(2x - 3) - 5| < \epsilon$$

$$-\epsilon < 2x - 8 < \epsilon$$

$$-\epsilon + 8 < 2x < \epsilon + 8$$

$$\frac{-\epsilon + 8}{2} < x < \frac{\epsilon + 8}{2}$$

$$\frac{-\epsilon + 8}{2} - 2 < x - 2 < \frac{\epsilon + 8}{2} - 2$$

$$-\frac{\epsilon + 4}{2} < \frac{-\epsilon + 4}{2} < x - 2 < \frac{\epsilon + 4}{2}$$

$$\delta = \frac{\epsilon + 4}{2}$$

To check it, we plug δ back in to try to solve for ε again.

$$|x - 2| < \frac{\epsilon + 4}{2}$$

$$-\frac{\epsilon + 4}{2} < x - 2 < \frac{\epsilon + 4}{2}$$

$$-(\epsilon + 4) < 2x - 4 < \epsilon + 4$$

$$-(\epsilon + 8) < 2x - 8 < \epsilon < \epsilon + 8$$

$$|(2x - 3) - 5| < \epsilon + 8$$

Since we are unable to conclude the original ε equation, the limit thus does not exist at 5.

13

CHAPTER 2 - DIFFERENTIATION

2.1 - The Definition of the Derivative

The **derivative** of a function is simply the slope of the tangent line to a function at a point. *Remember what the derivative represents - it's crucial to understand this later on.*

But how do you find that slope with only one point? You need two points to find a slope...

Let's start by approximating it using a secant line, or a line that intersects a curve.

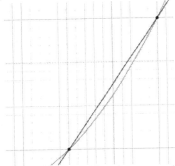

The first point is at $(x, f(x))$, and let the second point be at $(x + \Delta x, f(x + \Delta x))$. Using the slope equation, we find that the secant line's slope is equal to

$$\frac{f(x + \Delta x) - f(x)}{(x + \Delta x) - x} = \frac{f(x + \Delta x) - f(x)}{\Delta x}$$

Now imagine if we were to decrease Δx, making the value of $x + \Delta x$ closer and closer to x...

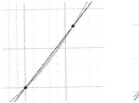  

As Δx gets closer and closer to 0, the secant line becomes a better and better approximation of the tangent line! However, realize that we can't just make Δx equal 0, since that would cause division by 0 in the slope equation.

But since Δx is getting infinitesimally close to 0, we can actually use a limit to approximate the slope of the tangent line using the equation for the slope of the secant line.

$$\lim_{\Delta x \to 0} \frac{f(x + \Delta x) - f(x)}{\Delta x}$$

And this is the **limit definition of a derivative**. This concept is extremely important, so remember it and ingrain it into your mind; the derivative is one of the fundamental concepts of calculus. We call taking the derivative of a function **differentiating** the function (please don't say "derivativing").

EXAMPLE 2.1.1:

Using the limit definition of the derivative, find the derivative of

$$f(x) = x^2.$$

$$\lim_{\Delta x \to 0} \frac{f(x + \Delta x) - f(x)}{\Delta x} = \lim_{\Delta x \to 0} \frac{(x + \Delta x)^2 - (x)^2}{\Delta x} =$$

$$\lim_{\Delta x \to 0} \frac{x^2 + 2\Delta x \cdot x + \Delta x^2 - x^2}{\Delta x} =$$

$$\lim_{\Delta x \to 0} \frac{2x\Delta x + \Delta x^2}{\Delta x} = \lim_{\Delta x \to 0} 2x + \Delta x = \boxed{2x}$$

Let's talk about differentiability now. Quite obviously, not all equations can be differentiated at every point. For instance, what would be the slope of the floor function at $x = 1$? Or the slope of the absolute value function at $x = 0$?

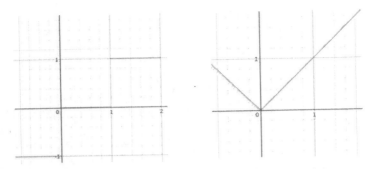

It suffices to say that we simply cannot differentiate those functions at those points. The **differentiability** of a function at a point is simply whether it can be differentiated at that point. In order for a function f to be differentiable at $x = c$, f must satisfy two conditions:

1. f must be continuous at c.
2. The derivative from the left of f at c must equal the derivative from the right of f of c.

If the function is continuous at a point, but derivatives from both sides of the equation don't equal each other at that point, there is a **cusp** at that point, where the derivative suddenly changes.

EXAMPLE 2.1.2:

Show that the function $f(x) = |x - 2|$ is not differentiable at $x = 2$.

1. *$f(x)$ is continuous; the limit as $f(x)$ approaches 2 is 0, and $f(2) = 0$.*
2. *However, the derivative from the left of f at $2 = -1$, and the derivative from the right of f at $2 = 1$. Since $-1 \neq 1$, $f(x)$ cannot be differentiated at $x = 2$ because there is a cusp there.*

Since a function must be continuous for it to be differentiable, differentiability implies continuity. However, as shown by the absolute value function, a function can be continuous but still not differentiable, so continuity does not imply differentiability.

16

TL;DR: If a function is differentiable at a point, then it must be continuous there, and have no cusp there.

Note: We use many different notations to represent a derivative. A derivative of function y can be seen as:

$$\frac{dy}{dx}$$

This one should make sense. It's a slope, so representing it is simply change in y over change in x.

$$y'; y'(x)$$

This one's easy to remember. Just put a little mark after the function name, and call it "y prime".

Later, we'll see that higher-order derivatives will be represented like so:

$$\frac{d^2y}{dx^2}; y''; y''(x)$$

And finally, solely $\frac{d}{dx}$ means to take the derivative (with respect to x) of the following expression.

There's just three more things to take note of when looking at derivatives and slope.

Horizontal tangents have a slope of 0. This means that when the derivative of a function is 0, we know that there's a horizontal tangent there. *(We'll see why how to use this later, in Section 3.3.)*

Vertical tangents have an *undefined* slope. This is because in a vertical line, the change in x, or dx, is 0, so the slope dy/dx would be undefined (division by 0).

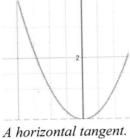

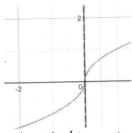

A horizontal tangent. *A vertical tangent.*

And finally, a **normal line** is a line perpendicular to the tangent line. Recall that lines perpendicular to each other have slopes that are negative reciprocals of each other.

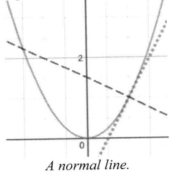

A normal line.

2.2 - Basic Derivative Rules

Now, I'll talk about a few rules that will make taking derivatives less painful than having to go through the limit definition every time.

The first rule you should know is the **Constant Rule**. It's really simple. Given constant c,

$$\frac{d}{dx}c = 0$$

It makes sense, right? A function $y = c$ is simply a horizontal line, and the slope of a horizontal line is always 0. Here's a short proof, though.

$$\frac{d}{dx}c = \lim_{\Delta x \to 0} \frac{c - c}{\Delta x} = 0$$

EXAMPLE 2.2.1:

Differentiate $\tan\left(\dfrac{37\pi}{9}\right)$.

$$\frac{d}{dx}\tan\left(\frac{37\pi}{9}\right) = \boxed{0}$$

It looks complicated, but it's just a constant.

The next rule is the **Constant Multiple Rule**. It's also fairly intuitive. Given a constant c and differentiable function f,

$$\frac{d}{dx}c \cdot f(x) = c \cdot \frac{d}{dx}f(x)$$

Again, the proof is very short:

$$\frac{d}{dx}c \cdot f(x) = \lim_{\Delta x \to 0} \frac{c \cdot f(x + \Delta x) - c \cdot f(x)}{\Delta x} =$$

$$\lim_{\Delta x \to 0} \frac{(c)(f(x + \Delta x) - f(x))}{\Delta x} = c \cdot \lim_{\Delta x \to 0} \frac{f(x + \Delta x) - f(x)}{\Delta x} =$$

$$c \cdot f'(x)$$

EXAMPLE 2.2.2:

Differentiate $2x^2$.

$$\frac{d}{dx}2x^2 = 2\frac{d}{dx}x^2 = 2(2x) = \boxed{4x}$$

19

We went through the derivative of x^2 in the last section, through the definition of the derivative. It's the same!

The **Sum Rule** is easy to remember, as well. Given two differentiable functions f and g:

$$\frac{d}{dx}[f(x) + g(x)] = \frac{d}{dx}f(x) + \frac{d}{dx}g(x)$$

And the proof:

$$\frac{d}{dx}[f(x) + g(x)] = \lim_{\Delta x \to 0} \frac{[f(x + \Delta x) + g(x + \Delta x)] - [f(x) + g(x)]}{\Delta x} =$$

$$\lim_{\Delta x \to 0}\left[\frac{f(x + \Delta x) - f(x)}{\Delta x} + \frac{g(x + \Delta x) - g(x)}{\Delta x}\right] =$$

$$\lim_{\Delta x \to 0}\frac{f(x + \Delta x) - f(x)}{\Delta x} + \lim_{\Delta x \to 0}\frac{g(x + \Delta x) - g(x)}{\Delta x} = f'(x) + g'(x)$$

EXAMPLE 2.2.3:

Differentiate $x^2 + 2$.

$$\frac{d}{dx}x^2 + 2 = \frac{d}{dx}x^2 + \frac{d}{dx}2 = 2x + 0 = \boxed{2x}$$

Now, we take a look at the **Power Rule**, one of the most useful rules in basic differentiation. For some number $n \neq 0$:

$$\frac{d}{dx}x^n = nx^{n-1}$$

Here's a proof of the Power Rule for positive integer n (although the Power Rule works for any real number $n \neq 0$). You're not expected to remember this, of course, but it's always nice to have some sort of proof to any formula you learn. Let $f(x) = x^n$.

$$f'(x) = \lim_{\Delta x \to 0} \frac{f(x + \Delta x) - f(x)}{\Delta x} = \lim_{\Delta x \to 0} \frac{(x + \Delta x)^n - x^n}{\Delta x} =$$

$$\lim_{\Delta x \to 0} \frac{\left(x^n + \binom{n}{1}x^{n-1}\Delta x^1 + \binom{n}{2}x^{n-2}\Delta x^2 + \cdots + \binom{n}{n-1}x^1\Delta x^{n-1} + \Delta x^n\right) - x^n}{\Delta x} =$$

$$\lim_{\Delta x \to 0} \frac{\binom{n}{1}x^{n-1}\Delta x^1 + \binom{n}{2}x^{n-2}\Delta x^2 + \cdots + \binom{n}{n-1}x^1\Delta x^{n-1} + \Delta x^n}{\Delta x} =$$

$$\lim_{\Delta x \to 0} \binom{n}{1}x^{n-1}\Delta x^0 + \binom{n}{2}x^{n-2}\Delta x^1 + \cdots + \binom{n}{n-1}x^1\Delta x^{n-2} + \Delta x^{n-1} =$$

$$\binom{n}{1}x^{n-1} = \boxed{nx^{n-1}}$$

EXAMPLE 2.2.4:

Differentiate x^5.
$$\frac{d}{dx}x^5 = \boxed{5x^4}$$

And finally, we have the **derivatives of sine and cosine**.
$$\frac{d}{dx}\sin(x) = \cos(x); \frac{d}{dx}\cos(x) = -\sin(x)$$
Proving these isn't actually that hard a task:

$$\frac{d}{dx}\sin(x) = \lim_{\Delta x \to 0} \frac{\sin(x + \Delta x) - \sin(x)}{\Delta x} =$$

$$\lim_{\Delta x \to 0} \frac{\sin(x)\cos(\Delta x) + \cos(x)\sin(\Delta x) - \sin(x)}{\Delta x} =$$

$$\lim_{\Delta x \to 0} \frac{\sin(x)(\cos(\Delta x) - 1) + \cos(x)\sin(\Delta x)}{\Delta x} =$$

$$\lim_{\Delta x \to 0} \sin(x)\frac{\cos(\Delta x) - 1}{\Delta x} + \cos(x)\frac{\sin(\Delta x)}{\Delta x} =$$

$$(\sin(x))(0) + (\cos(x))(1) = \boxed{\cos(x)}$$

Squeeze Theorem trig limits!

$$\frac{d}{dx}\cos(x) = \frac{d}{dx}\sin\left(x + \frac{\pi}{2}\right) =$$

$$\cos\left(x + \frac{\pi}{2}\right) = \boxed{-\sin(x)}$$

This proof assumes you already know the Chain Rule, which will be discussed in Section 2.4.

I'll give some more examples to strengthen your knowledge of these rules.

EXAMPLE 2.2.5:

Differentiate $x^2 - 2x + 1$.

$$\frac{d}{dx}x^2 - 2x + 1 = \frac{d}{dx}x^2 - 2\frac{d}{dx}x + \frac{d}{dx}1 = 2x - 2(1) + 0 = \boxed{2x - 2}.$$

EXAMPLE 2.2.6:

Differentiate $(2x^2 + 3)(5x - 1)$.

$$\frac{d}{dx}(2x^2 + 3)(5x - 1) = \frac{d}{dx}10x^3 - 2x^2 + 15x - 3 =$$

$$10\frac{d}{dx}x^3 - 2\frac{d}{dx}x^2 + 15\frac{d}{dx}x - \frac{d}{dx}3 = \boxed{30x^2 - 4x + 15}$$

EXAMPLE 2.2.7:

Differentiate $\dfrac{x^3 - 3x^2 - 4}{x^2}$.

$$\frac{d}{dx}\frac{x^3 - 3x^2 - 4}{x^2} = \frac{d}{dx}x - 3 - \frac{4}{x^2} = \frac{d}{dx}x - \frac{d}{dx}3 - 4\frac{d}{dx}x^{-2}$$

$$= 1 - 4(-2x^{-3}) = \boxed{1 + \frac{8}{x^3}}$$

EXAMPLE 2.2.8:

Differentiate $4x^5 - \cos(x)$.

$$\frac{d}{dx}4x^5 - \cos(x) = 4\frac{d}{dx}x^5 - \frac{d}{dx}\cos(x) = 4(5x^4) - (-\sin(x))$$

$$= \boxed{20x^4 + \sin(x)}$$

EXAMPLE 2.2.9: *A word problem!*
A rock is dropped from a height of 20 meters. Its position can be
represented by the equation
$s(t) = -5t^2 + 20$. What is the velocity of the rock at 1.5 seconds?
The velocity is simply the change in rate of position, or the
derivative of position!
$$s'(t) = v(t) = -10t$$
And now we plug in t = 1.5 sec.
$$v(1.5) = \textbf{-15 m/s}$$

A quick recap of the derivative rules in this chapter:

$$\frac{d}{dx}c = 0$$

$$\frac{d}{dx}c \cdot f(x) = c \cdot \frac{d}{dx}f(x)$$

$$\frac{d}{dx}[f(x) + g(x)] = \frac{d}{dx}f(x) + \frac{d}{dx}g(x)$$

$$\frac{d}{dx}x^n = nx^{n-1}$$

$$\frac{d}{dx}\sin(x) = \cos(x); \quad \frac{d}{dx}\cos(x) = -\sin(x)$$

2.3 - Product Rule and Quotient Rule

Now it's time to delve into more complicated derivative rules. We'll start with the **Product Rule**. Given two differentiable functions f and g:

$$\frac{d}{dx} f(x)g(x) = f'(x)g(x) + f(x)g'(x)$$

Since the proofs start getting really big, I'll only prove the Product Rule. Quotient Rule's proof is very similar.

EXAMPLE 2.3.1:

Differentiate $\sin(x)\cos(x)$.

$$\frac{d}{dx}\sin(x)\cos(x) = \left(\frac{d}{dx}\sin(x)\right)(\cos(x)) + (\sin(x))\left(\frac{d}{dx}\cos(x)\right) =$$

$$(\cos(x))(\cos(x)) + (\sin(x))(-\sin(x)) = \cos^2(x) - \sin^2(x) = \boxed{\cos(2x)}$$

Wow, what a nice answer.

The other rule in this section is the **Quotient Rule**. Given two differentiable functions f and g:

$$\frac{d}{dx}\frac{f(x)}{g(x)} = \frac{f'(x)g(x) - f(x)g'(x)}{[g(x)]^2}$$

EXAMPLE 2.3.2:

Differentiate $\tan(x)$.

$$\frac{d}{dx}\tan(x) = \frac{d}{dx}\frac{\sin(x)}{\cos(x)} = \frac{[\frac{d}{dx}\sin(x)][\cos(x)] - [\sin(x)][\frac{d}{dx}\cos(x)]}{\cos^2(x)}$$

$$\frac{\cos^2(x) + \sin^2(x)}{\cos^2(x)} = \frac{1}{\cos^2(x)} = \boxed{\sec^2(x)}$$

Take note that you shouldn't just blindly use the Product and Quotient Rules whenever you see a product or fraction. Refer to Examples 2.2.6 and 2.2.7; it's sometimes easier to simplify/expand and use one of the easier derivative rules.

The proof for the Product Rule is on the next page.

Proof of the Product Rule: Given function $h(x) = f(x)\, g(x)$,

$$h'(x) = \lim_{\Delta x \to 0} \frac{h(x + \Delta x) - h(x)}{\Delta x}$$

$$= \lim_{\Delta x \to 0} \frac{f(x + \Delta x)g(x + \Delta x) - f(x)g(x)}{\Delta x}$$

$$= \lim_{\Delta x \to 0} \frac{f(x + \Delta x)g(x + \Delta x) - f(x)g(x + \Delta x) + f(x)g(x + \Delta x) - f(x)g(x)}{\Delta x}$$

$$= \lim_{\Delta x \to 0} \frac{[f(x + \Delta x) - f(x)] \cdot g(x + \Delta x) + f(x) \cdot [g(x + \Delta x) - g(x)]}{\Delta x}$$

$$= \lim_{\Delta x \to 0} \frac{f(x + \Delta x) - f(x)}{\Delta x} \cdot \lim_{\Delta x \to 0} g(x + \Delta x) + \lim_{\Delta x \to 0} f(x) \cdot \lim_{\Delta x \to 0} \frac{g(x + \Delta x) - g(x)}{\Delta x}$$

$$= f'(x)g(x) + f(x)g'(x).$$

2.4 - The Chain Rule

The last derivative rule we learn is the **Chain Rule**. It takes the derivative of a composition of functions, or functions inside functions. Given differentiable functions f and g:

$$\frac{d}{dx}f(g(x)) = f'(g(x))g'(x)$$

Huh? What does that mean? Here, have an example that might clarify things:

EXAMPLE 2.4.1:

Differentiate $\sqrt{x^2 + 1}$.
$$f(x) = \sqrt{x}\ ;\ g(x) = x^2 + 1$$
Notice how $f(g(x))$ equals the original equation.

$$\frac{d}{dx}\sqrt{x^2 + 1} = f'(g(x))g'(x) = f'(x^2+1)g'(x) = \frac{1}{2\sqrt{x^2+1}} \cdot 2x$$

$$= \boxed{\frac{x}{\sqrt{x^2+1}}}$$

What just happened? We first took the derivative of the outer function f, the square root, and then plugged in inner function g.

$$f'(x) = \frac{1}{2\sqrt{x}} \implies f'(x^2+1) = \frac{1}{2\sqrt{x^2+1}}$$

Then, we multiplied it by the derivative of the inner function g.

$$g'(x) = 2x$$

And that's it! You now have differentiated using Chain Rule.

The Chain Rule is nice in the fact that it has a pretty simple and intuitive "proof":

$$\frac{df}{dx} = \frac{df}{dg}\frac{dg}{dx} = f'(g) \cdot g'(x) = f'(g(x))g'(x)$$

You can also apply the Chain Rule for compositions of more than two functions, too! Just keep taking the derivative of each successive outside function until you get to the inner one.

EXAMPLE 2.4.2:

Differentiate $\sin((x^2 - 1)^5)$.
Tip: Don't expand that fifth power.
$$\cos((x^2 - 1)^5) \cdot 5(x^2 - 1)^4 \cdot 2x$$

26

2.5 - Implicit Differentiation

So up until now, all functions have been defined explicitly, meaning the function is written in terms of x.

$$y = 2x + 1$$

An explicitly defined function y of x.

And we know how to take the derivative of these.

But how about equations where y isn't explicitly defined in terms of x? For example:

$$x^2 - 2y^3 + 4y = 2$$

An implicitly defined y.

How would you find $\frac{dy}{dx}$ of this equation? You can't really just solve for y as a function of x here. So instead, you use **implicit differentiation**. This means that we take the derivative of both sides of this equation *with respect to x*. Here's an example.

Note: when you do implicit differentiation you are assuming that y is differentiable with respect to x.

EXAMPLE 2.5.1:

Given $x^2 - 2y^3 + 4y = 2$, find $\frac{dy}{dx}$.

Let's take the derivative of both sides with respect to x.

$$\frac{d}{dx}x^2 - 2y^3 + 4y = \frac{d}{dx}2$$

$$\frac{d}{dx}x^2 - 2\frac{d}{dx}y^3 + 4\frac{d}{dx}y = 0$$

Since we're differentiating with respect to x, realize that we have to use the chain rule when dealing with y! Let's practice with the second term.

$$-2\frac{d}{dx}y^3$$

The outer function is x^3 and the inner function is y. Do you see it?

$$-2 \cdot 3y^2 \cdot \frac{dy}{dx}$$

So we use the chain rule to take that derivative. Remember that dy/dx stands for the derivative of y with respect to x. Let's continue with the full equation now.

$$2x - 6y^2\frac{dy}{dx} + 4\frac{dy}{dx} = 0$$

$$2x = 6y^2\frac{dy}{dx} - 4\frac{dy}{dx}$$

27

$$\frac{dy}{dx} = \frac{2x}{6y^2 - 4}$$

Notice that the formula for the derivative of that function requires both an x and y value. To better understand this, let's take a look at the graph of this equation.

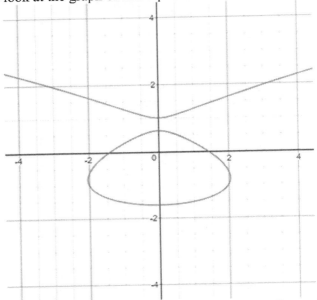

Of course, it's clear that y isn't actually a <u>function</u> of x, so the slope at a specific x might not be the same for different value of y. However, you can still find the slope of the tangent line at any point (x, y) from the equation of the derivative.

EXAMPLE 2.5.2:

For $x^2 - 2y^3 + 4y = 2$, find the slope of the tangent line at $(0, 1)$.
Just looking at the graph, we can guess that the slope is 0. However, let's plug it in to check.

$$\frac{dy}{dx} = \frac{2x}{6y^2 - 4}$$

$$\left.\frac{dy}{dx}\right|_{\substack{x=0 \\ y=1}} = \frac{2(0)}{6(1)^2 - 4} = \boxed{0}$$

28

Note: that vertical line there is called an evaluation line. You use it to say what values to put in.

Furthermore, using implicit differentiation, I can now offer you a proof of the Power Rule for any rational power n. (A bit off topic, but shows how cool implicit is.) Assume p and q are integers:

$$y = x^{\frac{p}{q}} \implies y^q = x^p \implies \frac{d}{dx}y^q = \frac{d}{dx}x^p$$

$$\implies qy^{q-1} \cdot \frac{dy}{dx} = px^{p-1} \implies$$

$$\frac{dy}{dx} = \frac{px^{p-1}}{qy^{q-1}} = \frac{p}{q}\frac{x^{p-1}}{x^{\frac{p}{q}(q-1)}} = \frac{p}{q}\frac{x^{p-1}}{x^{p-\frac{p}{q}}} = \frac{p}{q}x^{(p-1)-(p-\frac{p}{q})}$$

$$\boxed{= \frac{p}{q}x^{\frac{p}{q}-1}}$$

We can also use implicit differentiation and Chain Rule to find the derivatives of inverse functions! Let's see how.

EXAMPLE 2.5.3:

Differentiate $\arcsin(x)$.

Let's set $y = arcsin(x)$.

$$y = \arcsin(x) \implies \sin(y) = x$$

Now differentiate both sides with respect to x.

$$\frac{d}{dx}\sin(y) = \frac{d}{dx}x$$

$$\cos(y) \cdot \frac{dy}{dx} = 1$$

$$\frac{dy}{dx} = \frac{1}{\cos(y)}$$

Let's write this in terms of x, though. Recall that $sin^2(x) + cos^2(x) = 1$.

$$\frac{dy}{dx} = \frac{1}{\cos(y)} = \boxed{\frac{1}{\sqrt{1-x^2}}}$$

2.6 - Inverse Functions

An **inverse function** is a "reverse" of a function. It maps the outputs to the inputs of the original function. Generally, you can find the inverse of a function by flipping the function over $y = x$.

A function $f(x)$ only has an inverse function $f^{-1}(x)$ if it is **monotonic**. This means that its derivative does not change sign: it either never increases or never decreases. You can check if a function is monotonic with the horizontal line test. If you can draw a horizontal line that passes through multiple points, then the function is not monotonic.

What if we want to find the derivative of the inverse of a function? There's actually a fairly simple formula for this:

$$\frac{d}{dx}f^{-1}(x) = \frac{1}{f'(f^{-1}(x))}$$

Why does this formula work? The rigorous proof is difficult and convoluted, but there's a simple geometric proof I will show below.

First consider two lines that are inverses of each other. They should also be the reflections of each other over $y = x$.

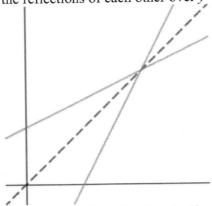

They have slopes that are reciprocals of each other. Keep this in mind. Now we're going to look at a function $f(x)$ and its inverse.

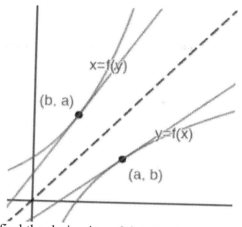

We want to find the derivative of $f(y)$, the inverse, at some $x = b$. We know that this derivative is the reciprocal of the slope of $f(x)$ at $x = a$.

$$\frac{d}{dx}f^{-1}(b) = \frac{1}{f'(a)}$$

But we also know that $a = f^{-1}(b)$! So we substitute this in, and we get:

$$\frac{d}{dx}f^{-1}(b) = \frac{1}{f'(f^{-1}(b))} \implies \frac{d}{dx}f^{-1}(x) = \frac{1}{f'(f^{-1}(x))}$$

Great! Let's go through some examples now.

EXAMPLE 2.6.1:

Given $f(2) = 5$, $f'(2) = 4$, $f(5) = 3$, and $f'(5) = 1$, calculate $(f^{-1})'(5)$.

We'll start off by plugging 5 into the formula.

$$(f^{-1})'(5) = \frac{1}{f'(f^{-1}(5))}$$

Notice that f(2) = 5, so f⁻¹(5) = 2!

$$(f^{-1})'(5) = \frac{1}{f'(2)} = \boxed{\frac{1}{4}}$$

EXAMPLE 2.6.2:

31

Given $f(x) = x^3 + x$, find $(f^{-1})'(0)$.

x = 0 is the only value of x that satisfies f(x) = 0.

$$(f^{-1})'(0) = \frac{1}{f'(f^{-1}(0))} = \frac{1}{f'(0)} = \frac{1}{3(0)^2 + 1} = \boxed{1}$$

EXAMPLE 2.6.3:

Find the derivative of $\arcsin(x)$.

$$\frac{d}{dx}\sin^{-1}(x) = \boxed{\frac{1}{\cos(\arcsin(x))}}$$

Remember, this can be simplified. Can you see how?

2.7 - Related Rates

Related rates is an application of implicit differentiation. After all this pure math, it's nice to figure out what we can do with derivatives in real life.

For related rates problems, it's best to just jump into a problem and see how it works. I'll explain the process as we go along.

EXAMPLE 2.7.1:

A 15 foot ladder is resting against the wall. The bottom is initially 10 feet away from the wall and is being pushed towards the wall at a rate of 0.25 ft/sec. How fast is the top of the ladder moving up the wall 4 seconds after we start pushing?

The first thing we want to note is that there are three variables in this equation.

Let y represent how high up the top of the ladder is, let x represent how far the bottom of the ladder is away from the wall, and let t represent the number of seconds elapsed.

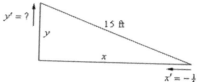

Here's a diagram to depict what I'm talking about. It's generally a good idea to draw a picture when doing related rates problems so the variables don't get jumbled around in your head.

Now that we have the variables set up, we need to find an equation relating x and y. Let's use the Pythagorean Theorem for this right triangle.

$$x^2 + y^2 = 225$$

And now we differentiate both sides implicitly with respect to time.

$$\frac{d}{dt}x^2 + y^2 = \frac{d}{dt}225 \implies 2x\frac{dx}{dt} + 2y\frac{dy}{dt} = 0$$

From the equation relating two variables we now have an equation relating two rates, or how fast x and y are changing! Now, to find the answer to our question:

dx/dt = -0.25 ft/sec *(it's negative because x is getting smaller)*
$$x = 10 \text{ ft} - 0.25 \text{ ft/sec} * 4 \text{ sec} = 9 \text{ ft}$$
$$y = 12 \text{ ft } \textit{(through the Pythagorean Theorem)}$$
$$2x\frac{dx}{dt} + 2y\frac{dy}{dt} = 0 \implies 2(9)(-0.25) + 2(12)\left(\frac{dy}{dt}\right) = 0 \implies \boxed{\frac{dy}{dt} = \frac{3}{16} \text{ ft/sec}}$$

At t = 4 seconds, the ladder is moving up the wall at a rate of 0.1875 ft/sec.

In essence, given an equation relating two variables, we can find a relationship between the rates of those two variables. This opens up many possible types of problems that can be solved with this method. Since I've already shown an example, I'll go through these examples more quickly.

Triangle angle problems.

EXAMPLE 2.7.2:

A lighthouse is 500 meters away from shore. Its light rotates at 2 revolutions per minute. When the light beam makes an angle of 30 degrees with the line perpendicular from the lighthouse to the shore, how fast is the light beam moving along the shore?

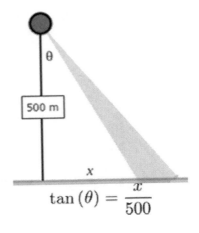

$$\tan(\theta) = \frac{x}{500}$$

$$\frac{d}{dt}\tan(\theta) = \frac{d}{dt}\frac{x}{500} \implies \sec^2(\theta)\frac{d\theta}{dt} = \frac{1}{500}\frac{dx}{dt}$$

Recall that we found the derivative of tangent in Section 2.3. If you don't remember, just use quotient rule.

$$\theta = \pi/6 \ radians$$
$$d\theta/dt = 2 \ rev/min = 4\pi \ rad/min$$

$$\sec^2(\theta)\frac{d\theta}{dt} = \frac{1}{500}\frac{dx}{dt} \implies \sec^2\left(\frac{\pi}{6}\right)\cdot 4\pi = \frac{1}{500}\frac{dx}{dt}$$

$$\implies \left(\frac{2}{\sqrt{3}}\right)^2 \cdot 4\pi = \frac{1}{500}\frac{dx}{dt} \implies \boxed{\frac{dx}{dt} = \frac{8000\pi}{3} \ m/min}$$

Area problems.

EXAMPLE 2.7.3:

A fire is spreading through a forest in a circle. The radius of this circle is increasing at a rate of 1 meter per minute. When the radius of the fire is 10 meters, how fast is the amount of burning area increasing?

$$A = \pi r^2$$

$$\frac{d}{dt}A = \frac{d}{dt}\pi r^2 \implies \frac{dA}{dt} = 2\pi r\frac{dr}{dt}$$

$$r = 10 \text{ meters}$$
$$dr/dt = 1 \text{ m/min}$$

$$\frac{dA}{dt} = 2\pi \frac{dr}{dt} \implies \frac{dA}{dt} = 2\pi(10)(1) \implies \boxed{\frac{dA}{dt} = 20\pi \text{ m}^2/\text{min}}$$

Volume problems. (Remember your formulas!)

EXAMPLE 2.7.4:

A sand leak forms a conical pile of sand with $r = 3h$. Sand is falling at a rate of 9 m³/hr. When the pile is 1 meter high, how quickly is the radius of the base of the cone increasing?

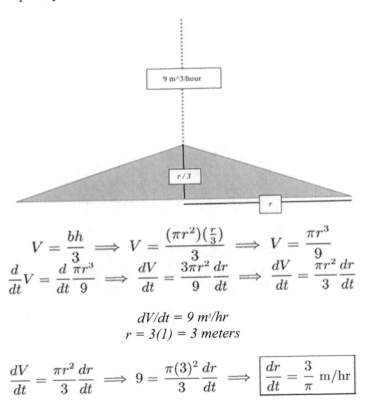

9 m^3/hour

r/3

r

$$V = \frac{bh}{3} \implies V = \frac{(\pi r^2)(\frac{r}{3})}{3} \implies V = \frac{\pi r^3}{9}$$

$$\frac{d}{dt}V = \frac{d}{dt}\frac{\pi r^3}{9} \implies \frac{dV}{dt} = \frac{3\pi r^2}{9}\frac{dr}{dt} \implies \frac{dV}{dt} = \frac{\pi r^2}{3}\frac{dr}{dt}$$

$$dV/dt = 9 \text{ m}^3/hr$$
$$r = 3(1) = 3 \text{ meters}$$

$$\frac{dV}{dt} = \frac{\pi r^2}{3}\frac{dr}{dt} \implies 9 = \frac{\pi(3)^2}{3}\frac{dr}{dt} \implies \boxed{\frac{dr}{dt} = \frac{3}{\pi} \text{ m/hr}}$$

Shadow problems.

EXAMPLE 2.7.5:

A 5 foot man walks away from a 12 foot lamp at a rate of 4 feet per second. If his shadow is 10 feet long, how quickly is his shadow lengthening?

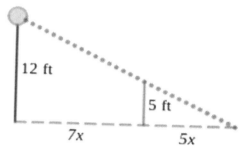

We know that the man is moving at 4 feet per second, so

$$\frac{d}{dt}7x = 7\frac{dx}{dt} = 4 \implies \frac{dx}{dt} = \frac{4}{7}$$

Now calculate the rate of change of the length of the shadow.

$$\frac{d}{dt}5x = 5\frac{dx}{dt} = 5\left(\frac{4}{7}\right) = \boxed{\frac{20}{7} \text{ ft/s}}$$

Notice that we didn't use the value of the length of the shadow at all to get our final answer! This is because since length of shadow and distance from lamp are directly related; it doesn't matter how long his shadow or how far away he is from the lamp, the rate of change of shadow length will be the same for a given walking speed.

2.8 - Differentiating the Natural Logarithm

The **natural logarithm** is a logarithm with base e. The natural log, denoted by the symbol **ln**, has a special derivative:

$$\frac{d}{dx} \ln x = \frac{1}{x}$$

I won't go into a proof for now, since it requires knowing the derivative of e^x, which is the next section.

EXAMPLE 2.8.1:

Differentiate $\ln(3x)$.

$$\frac{d}{dx} \ln(3x) = \frac{1}{3x} \cdot 3 = \boxed{\frac{1}{x}}$$

Can't forget the Chain Rule!

Notice something interesting? The derivative of $\ln(3x)$ is the same as the derivative of $\ln(x)$! Unfortunately, this doesn't hold true for all variations of ln functions.

EXAMPLE 2.8.2:

Differentiate $\ln(x^2 + 1)$.

$$\frac{d}{dx} \ln(x^2 + 1) = \frac{1}{x^2 + 1} \cdot 2x = \boxed{\frac{2x}{x^2 + 1}}$$

But the pattern should be pretty apparent: just put the inner function in the denominator and the derivative in the numerator.

EXAMPLE 2.8.3:

Differentiate $\ln(\sin(x))$.

$$\frac{d}{dx} \ln(\sin(x)) = \frac{1}{\sin(x)} \cdot \cos(x) = \frac{\cos(x)}{\sin(x)} = \boxed{\cot(x)}$$

Interesting.

There's also a cool differentiation trick called **logarithmic differentiation**. This is used when there are functions raised to the power of other functions. The idea is that when you take the logarithm of a function, you can put the power in front of the logarithm.

$$\ln(x^a) = a\ln(x)$$

So by setting the function to some *y* and then taking the natural log of both sides, you can eliminate the exponent, using the Product Rule on the resulting expression. Let's run through an example.

EXAMPLE 2.8.4:

Differentiate x^x.

Let's set this equal to y, then take the natural log of both sides.

$$y = x^x \implies \ln(y) = \ln(x^x) = x\ln(x)$$

Now differentiate both sides with respect to x. Pay attention to the Chain Rule on y!

$$\frac{1}{y} \cdot \frac{dy}{dx} = x \cdot \frac{1}{x} + 1 \cdot \ln(x)$$

$$\frac{dy}{dx} = (1 + \ln(x)) \cdot y$$

Now substitute the original y back into the equation, and you've solved for dy/dx!

$$\frac{dy}{dx} = \boxed{(1 + \ln(x)) \cdot x^x}$$

One more example, with weirder functions now.

EXAMPLE 2.8.5:

Differentiate $\sec(x)^{\cot(x)}$.

We can still use the same strategy.

$$y = \sec(x)^{\cot(x)} \implies \ln(y) = \cot(x)\ln(\sec(x))$$

$$\frac{1}{y} \cdot \frac{dy}{dx} = \cot(x) \cdot \frac{1}{\sec(x)} \cdot \sec(x)\tan(x) + (-\csc^2(x)) \cdot \ln(\sec(x))$$

Chain Rule! Can't forget that.

$$\frac{dy}{dx} = (1 - \csc^2(x) \cdot \ln(\sec(x))) \cdot y$$

$$\frac{dy}{dx} = \boxed{(1 - \csc^2(x) \cdot \ln(\sec(x))) \cdot \sec(x)^{\cot(x)}}$$

2.9 - Differentiating e^x

e^x is an interesting function: its derivative is itself!

$$\frac{d}{dx}e^x = e^x$$

We can prove this by using the inverse function formula on ln:

$$f(x) = \ln(x)$$

$$f^{-1}(x) = e^x$$

$$\frac{d}{dx}f^{-1}(x) = \frac{1}{\frac{1}{e^x}}$$

$$\frac{d}{dx}e^x = e^x$$

Let's run through an example.

EXAMPLE 2.9.1:

Differentiate e^{x^2}.

Chain Rule!

$$\frac{d}{dx}e^{x^2} = \boxed{e^{x^2} \cdot 2x}$$

2.10 - Exponentials and Logarithms with Other Bases

This really covers the same ideas as the previous few sections; these formulas work by just changing the base using exponent/log rules. Let's start with exponential functions.

Suppose we have an exponential with an arbitrary positive base, let's say, a.

$$a^x$$

How do we differentiate this? We can turn the a into a e expression using exponent properties:

$$a^x = \left(e^{\ln(a)}\right)^x = e^{x\ln(a)}$$

and now this can be differentiated using the Chain Rule.

$$\frac{d}{dx}e^{x\ln(a)} = \ln(a) \cdot e^x$$

Similarly, we can use the change-of-base formula for logarithms.

$$\log_a(x) = \frac{\ln(x)}{\ln(a)}$$

And again, easily differentiable.

$$\frac{d}{dx}\frac{\ln(x)}{\ln(a)} = \frac{1}{x\ln(a)}$$

2.11 - Parametric Derivatives

We'll start wrapping up this unit by delving just a bit further into derivatives.

Let's review the concept of parametric equations first, though. **Parametric equations** are when, instead of defining y in terms of x, we define y and x in terms of a third variable, the "parameter", which is usually t. For example:
$$y = 50x^2 + 1 \text{ vs. } y = 2t^2 + 1; x = \tfrac{t}{5}$$
These two actually define the same equation. Can you see how? *Hint: solve for t and plug it into the other equation.*

So how would you find dy/dx with parametric equations? It's actually very easy to remember:
$$\frac{dy}{dx} = \frac{\frac{dy}{dt}}{\frac{dx}{dt}}$$

EXAMPLE 2.11.1:
$$x = 2t^2 - 3t \qquad y = 2\sin(t)$$
Find the equation of the tangent line at $t = 1$.

$$\frac{dy}{dx} = \frac{\frac{dy}{dt}}{\frac{dx}{dt}} = \frac{2\cos(t)}{4t - 3}$$
The derivative of the parametric equation.
$$x\big|_{t=1} = 2(1)^2 - 3(1) = -1 \qquad y\big|_{t=1} = 2\sin(1)$$
The point (x, y) when t = 1.
$$\frac{dy}{dx}\bigg|_{t=1} = \frac{2\cos(1)}{4(1) - 3} = 2\cos(1)$$
The slope of the tangent line when t = 1.
$$\boxed{y - 2\sin(1) = 2\cos(1)(x + 1)}$$
And finally, just use point-slope form to find the equation.

You can also find the second derivative of a parametric equation.
$$\frac{d^2y}{dx^2} = \frac{\frac{d}{dt}\frac{dy}{dx}}{\frac{dx}{dt}}$$

The proof is slightly convoluted, but not that bad.

$$\frac{d}{dt}\frac{dy}{dx} = \frac{d}{dt}y'(x(t)) = y''(x(t)) \cdot x'(t) = \frac{d^2y}{dx^2}\frac{dx}{dt} \implies \frac{d^2y}{dx^2} = \frac{\frac{d}{dt}\frac{dy}{dx}}{\frac{dx}{dt}}$$

EXAMPLE 2.11.2:

$$x = 3 + 4\cos(\theta) \qquad y = 5 + 2\sin(\theta)$$

$$\text{Find } \frac{d^2y}{dx^2}.$$

$$\frac{dy}{dx} = \frac{2\cos(\theta)}{-4\sin(\theta)} = -\frac{1}{2}\cot(\theta)$$

$$\frac{d^2y}{dx^2} = \frac{\frac{1}{2}\csc^2(\theta)}{-4\sin(\theta)} = \boxed{-\frac{1}{2}\csc^3(\theta)}$$

2.12 - Polar Equations and Derivatives

I'll first go over a quick review of polar coordinates and graphs before I get into those derivatives.

Polar coordinates are in the form (r, θ). r and θ stand for radius and angle, respectively.

$$\left(2, \frac{\pi}{6}\right)$$

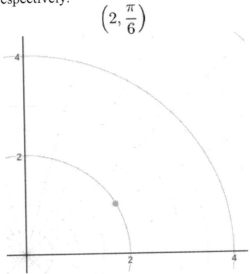

You can convert to Cartesian/rectangular coordinates using the following formulas:

$$x = r\cos(\theta) \quad y = r\sin(\theta) \quad x^2 + y^2 = r^2 \quad \frac{y}{x} = \tan(\theta)$$

Now for a quick review of common polar equations. *Note: You could also graph the equations by point plotting, but it's generally more efficient to just memorize the formulas.*

Circles.

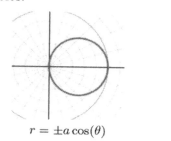

$$r = \pm a \cos(\theta)$$

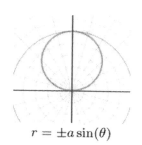

$$r = \pm a \sin(\theta)$$

a is the diameter of the circle.

Limaçons.

	$r = a \pm b \cos(\theta)$	$r = a \pm b \sin(\theta)$
$\dfrac{a}{b} < 1$		
$\dfrac{a}{b} = 1$		
$1 < \dfrac{a}{b} < 2$		
$\dfrac{a}{b} \geq 2$		

45

Careful! Limaçons have a cusp when a/b = 1! You can't take the derivative there.
When a/b < 1, the inner loop has size b - a, and the outer loop has size b + a.

Polar roses.

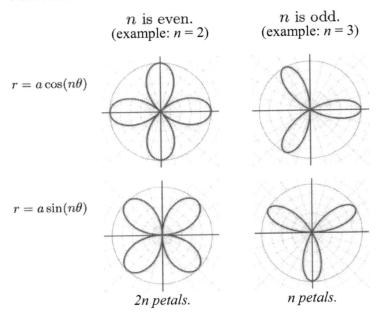

	n is even. (example: $n = 2$)	n is odd. (example: $n = 3$)
$r = a\cos(n\theta)$		
$r = a\sin(n\theta)$		
	2n petals.	*n petals.*

And finally, we get to polar derivatives. It's pretty much the same as parametric derivatives.

$$\frac{dy}{dx} = \frac{\frac{dy}{d\theta}}{\frac{dx}{d\theta}}$$

EXAMPLE 2.12.1:

$$r = 2 + 4\cos(\theta)$$

For what values of θ is the tangent line vertical over the interval $[0, 2\pi)$?

$$x = r\cos(\theta) = (2 + 4\cos(\theta))(\cos(\theta))$$
$$y = r\sin(\theta) = (2 + 4\cos(\theta))(\sin(\theta))$$

46

Now remember, a vertical tangent line has an undefined slope. So in order for the slope to be undefined here, dx/dθ has to equal 0.

$$\frac{dx}{d\theta} = (-4\sin(\theta))(\cos(\theta)) + (2+4\cos(\theta))(-\sin(\theta)) = -2\sin(\theta) - 8\sin(\theta)\cos(\theta)$$

Product rule!

$$-2\sin(\theta) - 8\sin(\theta)\cos(\theta) = 0 \implies (-2\sin(\theta))(1 + 4\cos(\theta)) = 0$$

$$\implies -2\sin(\theta) = 0; 1 + 4\cos(\theta) = 0$$

$$\implies \sin(\theta) = 0; \cos(\theta) = -\frac{1}{4}$$

$$\implies \boxed{\theta = 0, \arccos\left(-\frac{1}{4}\right), \pi, 2\pi - \arccos\left(-\frac{1}{4}\right)}$$

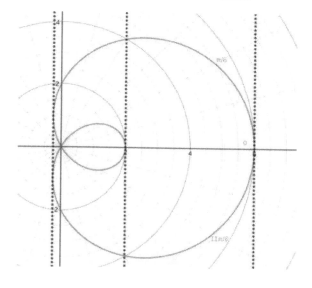

47

EXAMPLE 2.12.2:

Find the derivative of $r = 1 + \sin(\theta)$ at $\theta = \frac{3\pi}{2}$.

$$x = r\cos(\theta) = (1 + \sin(\theta))(\cos(\theta))$$
$$y = r\sin(\theta) = (1 + \sin(\theta))(\sin(\theta))$$

$$\frac{dy}{dx} = \frac{(\cos(\theta))(\sin(\theta)) + (1 + \sin(\theta))(\cos(\theta))}{(\cos(\theta))(\cos(\theta)) + (1 + \sin(\theta))(-\sin(\theta))}$$

$$\frac{dy}{dx}\bigg|_{\theta = \frac{3\pi}{2}} = \frac{(\cos(\frac{3\pi}{2}))(\sin(\frac{3\pi}{2})) + (1 + \sin(\frac{3\pi}{2}))(\cos(\frac{3\pi}{2}))}{(\cos(\frac{3\pi}{2}))(\cos(\frac{3\pi}{2})) + (1 + \sin(\frac{3\pi}{2}))(-\sin(\frac{3\pi}{2}))}$$

$$= \frac{(0)(-1) + (1 + (-1))(0)}{(0)(0) + (1 + (-1))(-(-1))} = \frac{0}{0} = \boxed{\text{DNE}}$$

What? Why is it 0/0? Let's take a look at the graph...

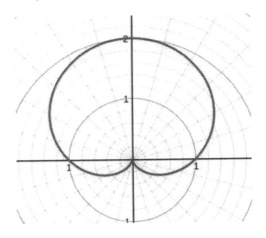

There's a cusp at exactly θ = 3π/2, so you can't take the derivative there!

CHAPTER 3 - DIFFERENTIATION APPLICATIONS

3.1 - Relative Extrema

So, what exactly *are* extreme values (or extrema)? Let's throw out some definitions first.

- $f(c)$ is the **absolute minimum of f** if $f(c) \leq f(x)$ for all x in the domain of f.
- $f(c)$ is the **absolute maximum of f** if $f(c) \geq f(x)$ for all x in the domain of f.
- $f(c)$ is a **relative minimum of f** if $f(c) \leq f(x)$ for all x in an open interval surrounding it.
- $f(c)$ is a **relative maximum of f** if $f(c) \geq f(x)$ for all x in an open interval surrounding it.

To visualize this, let's look at a graph of a function $a(x)$, defined over this very small interval:

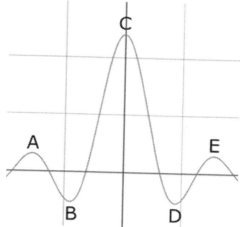

It's quite apparent point C is the absolute maximum of this function a, since it's higher than any other point on the function. B and D are both absolute minima (the plural for minimum), because there is no point that is lower than those two. And finally, A and E are relative maxima, because they are the highest point in their general vicinity, but not the highest point on the entire function.

It might to be helpful to think of relative maxima as on a "hill", and relative minima as in a "valley".

Furthermore, to locate an absolute extreme value, all you have to do is to check 1) the values of the two ends of the interval and 2) the values of any relative extrema. If the interval is open, i.e. not including endpoints, then just check the values of the relative extrema.

And finally, there is a theorem called the **Extreme Value Theorem**, or just EVT. It states that if function *f* is continuous on closed interval [*a*, *b*], then *f* has both a minimum and a maximum in that interval. *Remember those four theorems mentioned in Section 1.2? This is one of them!*

EXAMPLE 3.1.1:
Given the following graph, identify any extrema.

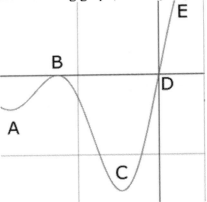

Point A is a relative minimum. Point B is a relative maximum. Point C is an absolute minimum. Point E is an absolute maximum.

We continue our discussion of extrema by examining critical points. Put simply, a **critical point** is a point on a function where the function is either not differentiable or the derivative there equals 0.

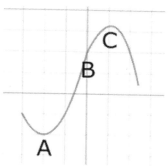

This function has three critical points: A and C because the derivative is 0, and B because there's a cusp at that point (not differentiable). Do you see the sharp part at B?

Do you see a relationship between critical points and extrema? A really important theorem can actually be drawn: that <u>relative extrema can only be found at critical points</u>. This is crucial, since this means that if a function is differentiable, then <u>any relative extrema have to have a slope of 0 or DNE</u>. *Remember when we talked about this in Section 2.1?*

We'll see how we can apply this new concept later in Section 3.3, but for now, just keep this piece of information about extrema in the back of your head as we go along.

3.2 - Rolle's Theorem and MVT

Let's introduce the last two of the four theorems, starting with
Rolle's Theorem, or RT for short.

RT says that
  If function f is continuous over [a, b], differentiable over (a, b),
    and f (a) = f (b), then there is at least one number c such that
                        f'(c) = 0.

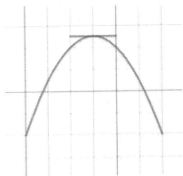

f'(c) = 0 is in blue on this graph.

EXAMPLE 3.2.1:

Find the two zeroes of the function $f(x) = x^2 - 3x + 2$ and show
that $f'(x) = 0$ at a point between them.

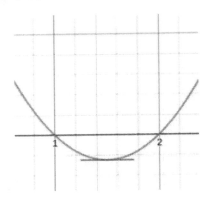

Through factoring, we see that the two zeroes are at x = 1 and x = 2. Since f(x) is continuous over [1, 2] and differentiable over (1, 2) and f(1) = f(2) = 0, through RT there must exist a number c such that f'(c) = 0.

But we really don't talk much about RT as we do about the **Mean Value Theorem**, or MVT, which is basically just a generalization of Rolle's.

MVT states that
If function f is continuous over [a, b] and differentiable over (a, b), then there is at least one number c such that

$$f'(c) = \frac{f(b) - f(a)}{b - a}.$$

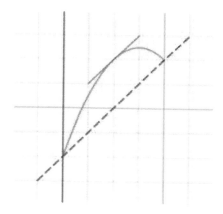

Notice that if $f(b) = f(a)$ then it's just Rolle's Theorem! But MVT is much more flexible, since it works for any a and b satisfying the continuity and differentiability conditions, guaranteeing the existence of a tangent line parallel to any secant line.

EXAMPLE 3.2.2:

A plane begins a 2500-mile flight at 2:00 PM. It arrives at its destination at 7:30 PM. Explain why there must have been at least two times during the flight that the plane was going at 400 mph.

Let s(t) be a function of miles traveled vs time. Assume s(t) is continuous over [2, 7.5] and differentiable over (2, 7.5). Thus, through MVT there must be some number 2 < c < 7.5 such that

$$f'(c) = \frac{f(7.5) - f(2)}{7.5 - 2} = \frac{2500}{5.5} \approx 454.54$$

. Then, assuming f'(2) = 0 and f'(7.5) = 0, through IVT there must be numbers 2 < a < c and c < b < 7.5 such that f'(a) = 400 and f'(b) = 400.

Again, note that we don't find exact values of a, b, or c; only that they exist.

3.3 - The First Derivative Test

Let's finally tie together derivatives and maxima. We've hinted at this before, but now we'll state it explicitly: **The First Derivative Test**.

Assume c is a critical point of function f.

1. If f' changes sign from positive to negative at c, then there is a relative maximum at c.
2. If f' changes sign from negative to positive at c, then there is a relative minimum at c.
3. If f' doesn't change sign at c, then there is neither a relative maximum nor minimum at c.

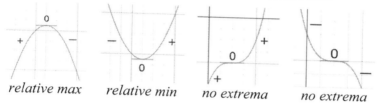

relative max *relative min* *no extrema* *no extrema*

We can model this behavior with **sign graphs**. A sign graph is basically a number line, but shows the sign (positive or negative) of the equation instead. We'll see how to use one in this example.

Let's go through the process of graphing an equation.

EXAMPLE 3.3.1:

Graph $f(x) = x^2 - 6x + 8$.

Let's start easy and find the y-intercept.
$$f(0) = 8.$$
(0, 8) is on the graph.

Now we'll find the zeroes.
$$x^2 - 6x + 8 = (x - 4)(x - 2) = 0$$
(2, 0) and (4, 0) are on the graph.

And finally we'll find any extrema.
$$f'(x) = 2x - 6$$

55

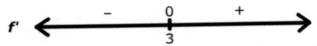

There is a relative minimum at x = 3 because the sign of f'
changes from negative to positive.
Plugging that in gives us f(3) = (3)² - 6(3) + 8 = -1. ⇒ (3, -1)

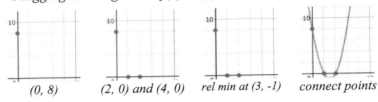

| (0, 8) | (2, 0) and (4, 0) | rel min at (3, -1) | connect points |

Alright, that problem was pretty easy. So now let's try applying
this concept to a harder question.

EXAMPLE 3.3.2:

$f(x)$ is a degree four polynomial equation satisfying the
following conditions:
(1, 2) is a relative minimum. (-1, 4) and (3, 4) are relative
maxima.
Find the equation of $f(x)$.

*Let's break this question apart. f(x) is of degree 4, so it has the
equation $ax^4 + bx^3 + cx^2 + dx + e$.
We know that f(1) = 2, f(-1) = 4, and f(3) = 4.
We also know that f'(1) = 0, f'(-1) = 0, and f'(3) = 0, since
they're relative maxima and thus have a derivative of 0.
Using the Power Rule, $f'(x) = 4ax^3 + 3bx^2 + 2cx + d$.*

So we can draw up a system of equations:
$$f(1) = a + b + c + d + e = 2$$
$$f(-1) = a - b + c - d + e = 4$$
$$f(3) = 81a + 27b + 9c + 3d + e = 4$$
$$f'(1) = 4a + 3b + 2c + d = 0$$
$$f'(-1) = -4a + 3b - 2c + d = 0$$
$$f'(3) = 108a + 27b + 6c + d = 0$$

Well, we can definitely solve that by hand, but we can use matrices on our calculators instead.

$$\text{rref}\left(\begin{bmatrix} 1 & 1 & 1 & 1 & 1 & 2 \\ 1 & -1 & 1 & -1 & 1 & 4 \\ 81 & 27 & 9 & 3 & 1 & 4 \\ 4 & 3 & 2 & 1 & 0 & 0 \\ -4 & 3 & -2 & 1 & 0 & 0 \\ 108 & 27 & 6 & 1 & 0 & 0 \end{bmatrix}\right) = \begin{bmatrix} 1 & 0 & 0 & 0 & 0 & -\frac{1}{8} \\ 0 & 1 & 0 & 0 & 0 & \frac{1}{2} \\ 0 & 0 & 1 & 0 & 0 & \frac{1}{4} \\ 0 & 0 & 0 & 1 & 0 & -\frac{3}{2} \\ 0 & 0 & 0 & 0 & 1 & \frac{23}{8} \\ 0 & 0 & 0 & 0 & 0 & 0 \end{bmatrix}$$

Reduced row echelon form saves the day! Notice that I just put the coefficients into the matrix.

The equation turns out to be $f(x) = -\frac{1}{8}x^4 + \frac{1}{2}x^3 + \frac{1}{4}x^2 - \frac{3}{2}x + \frac{23}{8}$.

3.4 - The Second Derivative Test

Just as the first derivative deals with the rate of change, the second derivative (or the derivative of the derivative) deals with the rate of rate of change, also known as **concavity**. If f' is increasing, or $f'' > 0$, then the function is concave up, and if f' is decreasing, or $f'' < 0$, then the function is concave down. You can think of concavity as the graph opening in a direction.

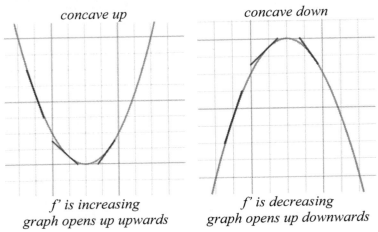

concave up   *concave down*

f' is increasing   *f' is decreasing*
graph opens up upwards   *graph opens up downwards*

Points of inflection are points where the concavity changes sign. Similar to relative extrema, points of inflection can only occur when *f''(x) = 0* or *f''(x)* does not exist.

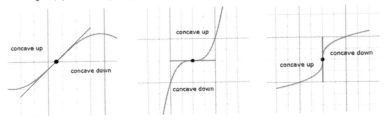

And we finally get to what the Second Derivative Test really is. Just like the First Derivative Test, it's a simple test that finds relative extrema. But, instead of using the first derivative, you use the second derivative.

The Second Derivative Test:
  Given that $f'(c) = 0$, and that f is twice differentiable at c:
    1. If $f''(c) > 0$, then $f(c)$ is a relative minimum.
    2. If $f''(c) < 0$, then $f(c)$ is a relative maximum.

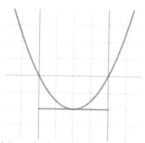   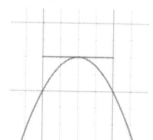

f'(c) = 0 (horizontal tangent)   *f'(c) = 0 (horizontal tangent)*
   f''(c) > 0 (concave up)   *f''(c) > 0 (concave up)*
     relative minimum   *relative maximum*

The Second Derivative Test is slightly easier than the First Derivative Test, since all you need to know is the sign of the second derivative, and not how it changes like when using the first derivative. However, the Second Derivative Test fails when $f''(c) = 0$, and when that happens, you have to resort to using the First Derivative Test. We'll finish up with an easy example.

EXAMPLE 3.4.1:
  Find the x-coordinates of all relative extrema of $x^3 + 6x^2 + 9x + 3$.

$$f'(x) = 3x^2 + 12x + 9 = 3(x + 3)(x + 1) = 0$$
$$f''(x) = 6x + 12$$

Since $f'(-1) = 0$ and $f''(-1) > 0$, there is a relative minimum at $x = -1$.
Since $f'(-3) = 0$ and $f''(-3) < 0$, there is a relative maximum at $x = -3$.

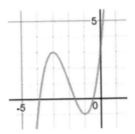

EXAMPLE 3.4.2:

Find the relative extrema of xe^x.

$$\frac{d}{dx}xe^x = (1)(e^x) + (x)(e^x) = (x+1)(e^x) = 0$$

$$x + 1 = 0 \implies x = -1$$

e^x can never equal 0, so we only check x+1.

Let's use the Second Derivative Test to check if it's a maximum or minimum.

$$\frac{d^2}{dx^2}xe^x = \frac{d}{dx}(x+1)(e^x) = (x+1)(e^x) + (1)(e^x) = (x+2)(e^x)$$

Plugging in x = −1, we see that the second derivative is greater than zero. Since f(x) is twice differentiable, has a horizontal tangent, and is concave up at x = 1, there is a relative minimum at x = −1.

3.5 - Limits at Infinity

Let's look at limits again. Up until now, we've only evaluated limits up to a finite number, like "as x approaches 2". But can we evaluate a limit if it goes to infinity?

Consider the graph of the function
$$\frac{3x^2 + 8}{x^2 + 1}$$

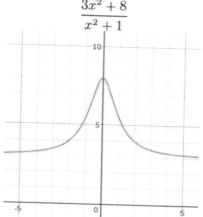

As x get larger and larger, or smaller and smaller, $f(x)$ gets closer to 3, but never touches it. So we can see that the end behavior of $f(x)$ is that it approaches 3, or expressed in limit form,

$$\lim_{x \to \infty} \frac{3x^2 + 8}{x^2 + 1} = 3; \quad \lim_{x \to -\infty} \frac{3x^2 + 8}{x^2 + 1} = 3$$

We can say that as x approaches infinity (or negative infinity), $f(x) = 3$.

But how do we find the value of this limit algebraically, or without looking at the graph or a table? It's actually really simple: just compare the highest degrees of the numerator and denominator.

You only care about the highest degree because when you get to really large numbers (approaching infinity), lower exponents don't really matter since the highest exponent gets so big.

Note: If a function is not a fraction, the lower degree is 0.

$$\frac{4x + 5}{4x^2 + 1}$$

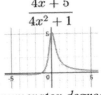

$$\frac{4x^2 + 5}{2x^2 + 1}$$

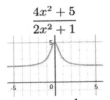

$$\frac{4x^3 + 5}{2x^2 + 1}$$

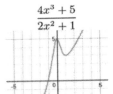

numerator degree smaller than denominator degree

numerator degree equal to denominator degree

numerator degree greater than denominator degree

limit at ±infinity equals 0

limit at ±infinity equals top coefficient over bottom coefficient, in this case 4/2

limit at ±infinity equals infinity or negative infinity

This chart is always true for rational functions. Note that if the limit at infinity equals a finite number, that number is that function's **horizontal asymptote**, since it approaches a value when going to infinity. *There is a third type of asymptote, oblique asymptotes, shown in the third graph. That'll be covered in the next section.*

EXAMPLE 3.5.1:

Find the horizontal asymptotes of a) $\dfrac{2x + 5}{2x^2 + 1}$ and b) $\dfrac{5x^5 + 7x^3 - 9}{2x^5 - 3}$.

a. Since the degree of the denominator (2) is higher than the degree of the numerator (1), the limit at infinity, or horizontal asymptote, equals 0.
b. Since the degree of the denominator (5) equals the degree of the numerator (5), divide the coefficient of the numerator (5) by the coefficient of the denominator (2).
The limit at infinity equals 5/2 = 2.5.

It's important to note that only *rational* functions fall into the above three categories. Functions that are *not* rational can actually have two horizontal asymptotes: one as *x* approaches infinity, and one as *x* approaches negative infinity.

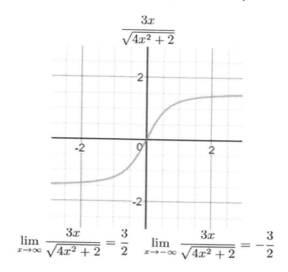

$$\lim_{x\to\infty} \frac{3x}{\sqrt{4x^2+2}} = \frac{3}{2} \qquad \lim_{x\to-\infty} \frac{3x}{\sqrt{4x^2+2}} = -\frac{3}{2}$$

Again, how do we find the limits without just looking at the graph? It's pretty similar to functions that are strictly rational, except we just need to check the sign of the horizontal tangent by plugging in positive and negative infinity. Here's an example to show what I mean.

EXAMPLE 3.5.2:

Find any horizontal asymptotes of the graph of $\dfrac{\sqrt{9x^6+3}}{x^3-2}$.

$$\frac{\sqrt{9x^6+3}}{x^3-2} \implies \frac{\sqrt{9x^6}}{x^3} \implies \frac{3x^3}{x^3} \implies 3$$

Now to check the sign.

$$\frac{\sqrt{9(\infty)^6}}{(\infty)^3} \implies \frac{3(\infty)^3}{(\infty)^3} \implies \frac{\text{positive}}{\text{positive}} \implies \text{positive}$$

As x approaches positive infinity, the horizontal tangent is at positive 3.

63

$$\frac{\sqrt{9(-\infty)^6}}{(-\infty)^3} \implies \frac{3\infty^3}{(-\infty)^3} \implies \frac{\text{positive}}{\text{negative}} \implies \text{negative}$$

As x approaches negative infinity, the horizontal tangent is at negative 3.

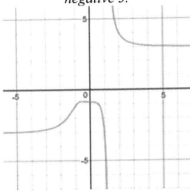

3.6 - Graphing Equations

Now it's time to use everything we've learned thus far to start graphing equations! A quick recap of what you'll need to know for this section:

- Vertical Asymptotes (Section 1.3)
- Derivatives and Differentiability (Section 2.1)
- Relative Extrema (Section 3.1 and Section 3.3)
- Sign Graphs (Section 3.3)
- Concavity (Section 3.4)
- Points of Inflection (Section 3.4)
- Horizontal Asymptotes (Section 3.5)

And oblique asymptotes, too! That'll be covered in this section. If any of the terms above seem confusing, go back and review them before proceeding.

We'll start off by graphing a simple equation.

EXAMPLE 3.6.1:

$$\text{Graph } x^3 - 6x^2 + 9x + 2.$$

We're going to start off by listing off everything we can find about this equation.

y-intercept: (0, 2)
x-intercept: (-0.196, 0)

First derivative: $3x^2 - 12x + 9$

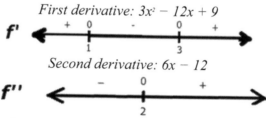

Second derivative: $6x - 12$

Concave up: x > 2, Concave down: x < 2

Through the Second Derivative Test we find that
Relative maxima: (1, 6) because concave down and horizontal tangent (c.d. and h.t.)
Relative minima: (3, 2) because concave up and horizontal tangent (c.u. and h.t.)

Points of inflection: (2, 4) because f'' changes sign at x = 2

No asymptotes.

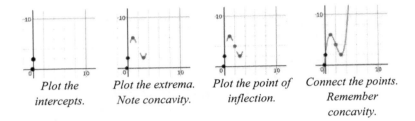

| Plot the intercepts. | Plot the extrema. Note concavity. | Plot the point of inflection. | Connect the points. Remember concavity. |

And that's pretty much the process of graphing equations! Just list out everything you know and connect them all together. I'll give a few more examples to show how this works.

EXAMPLE 3.6.2:

$$\text{Graph } \frac{6x^2 + 5}{3x - 1}.$$

y-intercept: (0, -5)
No x-intercept.
Vertical asymptote: x = 1/3

First derivative: $\dfrac{d}{dx} \dfrac{6x^2 + 5}{3x - 1} = \dfrac{(12x)(3x - 1) - (6x^2 + 5)(3)}{(3x - 1)^2}$

$$= \frac{36x^2 - 12x - 18x^2 - 15}{(3x - 1)^2} = \frac{3(6x^2 - 4x - 5)}{(3x - 1)^2}$$

f' $\xleftarrow{\hspace{1cm}}$ + 0 − ∅ − 0 + $\xrightarrow{\hspace{1cm}}$
                          -0.638   0.333   1.305

Second derivative: $\dfrac{d}{dx} \dfrac{3(6x^2 - 4x - 5)}{(3x - 1)^2}$

$$= 3 \cdot \frac{(12x - 4)(3x - 1)^2 - (6x^2 - 4x - 5)(2)(3x - 1)(3)}{(3x - 1)^4}$$

$$= 3 \cdot \frac{(36x^2 - 12x - 12x + 4) - (36x^2 - 24x - 30)}{(3x - 1)^3} = \frac{102}{(3x - 1)^3}$$

f'' $\xleftarrow{\hspace{1cm}}$ − ∅ + $\xrightarrow{\hspace{1cm}}$
                          0.333

Relative minima: (1.305, 5.221)
Relative maxima: (-0.638, -2.554)
No points of inflection or horizontal asymptotes.

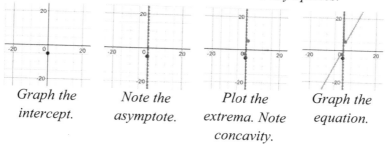

Graph the intercept.   *Note the asymptote.*   *Plot the extrema. Note concavity.*   *Graph the equation.*

This graph seems awfully suspicious. Even though there is no horizontal asymptote, the graph still seems to approach a straight line as x gets larger and larger.

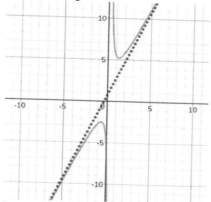

This is a special type of asymptote called an **oblique asymptote**. This happens whenever the degree of the numerator is larger than the degree of the denominator. (The limit at infinity goes to infinity, but it still follows a line.) You can find the equation of the oblique asymptote by long dividing and ignoring the remainder.

$$\frac{6x^2 + 5}{3x - 1} = 2x + \frac{2}{3} + \frac{\frac{17}{3}}{3x - 1} = 2x + \frac{2}{3}$$

For the rest of the examples, I'll stop showing work to save space. However, you should still be working these derivatives and graphs yourselves as practice.

EXAMPLE 3.6.3:

$$\text{Graph } \frac{4x^2 + 15}{12x - 5}.$$

y-intercept: (0, -3)
No x-intercept.
Vertical asymptote: x = 5/12
No horizontal asymptote.
Oblique asymptote: $\frac{1}{3}x + \frac{5}{36}$

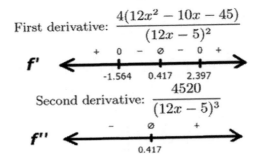

First derivative: $\dfrac{4(12x^2 - 10x - 45)}{(12x - 5)^2}$

Second derivative: $\dfrac{4520}{(12x - 5)^3}$

Relative minimum: (2.397, 1.598)
Relative maximum: (-1.564, -1.043)

No points of inflection.

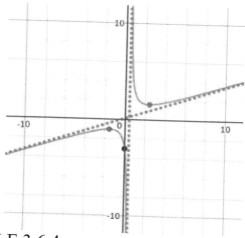

EXAMPLE 3.6.4:

Graph $\dfrac{x}{\sqrt{x^2 + 7}}$.

y-intercept: (0, 0)
x-intercept: (0, 0)
No vertical asymptotes.
Horizontal asymptotes: y = 1, y = -1

First derivative: $\dfrac{7}{(x^2 + 7)^{\frac{3}{2}}}$

$$f' \quad \xleftarrow{\qquad + \qquad} \longrightarrow$$

Second derivative: $-\dfrac{21x}{(x^2 + 7)^{\frac{5}{2}}}$

$$f'' \quad \xleftarrow{\quad + \quad} \underset{0}{|} \xrightarrow{\quad - \quad}$$

No relative extrema.
Concave up when x < 0, concave down when x > 0.

Point of inflection at (0, 0).

69

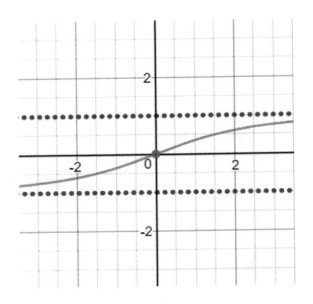

EXAMPLE 3.6.5:

$$\text{Graph } \frac{x^2 + x - 12}{x - 3}.$$

$$\frac{x^2 + x - 12}{x - 3} = \frac{(x + 4)(x - 3)}{x - 3} = x + 4, x \neq 3$$

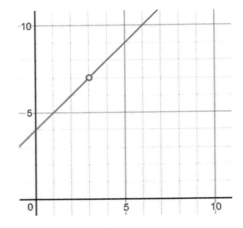

Always remember to simplify your expressions first!

3.7 - Optimization Problems

One of the most common applications of basic calculus is to find a minimum or maximum value, given some constraints, like finding "maximum area" or "minimum cost". There's really not much to explain, so let's just jump right into examples to give you a feel for the problems.

EXAMPLE 3.7.1:

Kim loves French fries. In fact, he loves them so much that he's been asked to design a new French fry box! The box must be a rectangular prism with an open top and must have a square base. Furthermore, he only has 108 square centimeters of cardboard to work with. How should Kim design the French fry box so that the box can contain the most French fries possible?

Let's note the important parts of the question.
1. *Open-topped rectangular prism with a square base.*
2. *The surface area of the rectangular prism must be 108 square centimeters.*
3. *The goal is to maximize the volume of the box.*

Let's also draw a diagram for this question.

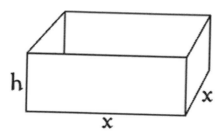

$$\text{Volume} = x^2 h$$
$$\text{Surface Area} = x^2 + 4xh = 108$$

We want to maximize volume, so let's try to express volume in terms of one variable only.

$$h = \frac{108 - x^2}{4x}$$

$$V = x^2\left(\frac{108 - x^2}{4x}\right) = 27x - \frac{1}{4}x^3$$

Great! We got V in terms of x. Now we just find its maximum value!

$$\frac{dV}{dx} = 27 - \frac{3}{4}x^2 = 0 \implies 3x^2 = 108 \implies x = 6$$

We ignore the negative value of x because x can't be negative in the context of this problem.

*The best dimensions for the box are thus **6×6×3**. (h = 3 when x = 6 from surface area equation.)*

EXAMPLE 3.7.2:

A farmer has 200 feet of fence. He wants to fence in two adjacent rectangular plots of land. What is the maximum area of land he can enclose?

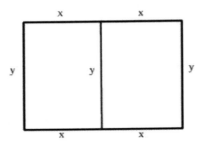

$$\text{Area} = 2xy$$
$$\text{Fence Length} = 4x + 3y = 200$$

Let's first put area in terms of one variable.

$$x = \frac{200 - 3y}{4}$$

$$A = 2y\left(\frac{200 - 3y}{4}\right) = 100y - \frac{3}{2}y^2$$

Then we'll find the maximum y.

$$\frac{dA}{dy} = 100 - 3y = 0 \implies 3y = 100 \implies y = \frac{100}{3}$$

And finally, just plug y back in to get the maximum area.

$$A = 100\left(\frac{100}{3}\right) - \frac{3}{2}\left(\frac{100}{3}\right)^2 = \boxed{\frac{5000}{3} \text{ square feet}}$$

As you can see, the problem solving part isn't hard; the difficult part is finding the right formulas.

3.8 - Newton's Method

Newton's Method is a recursive way to estimate a zero of an equation. Let's see how it works.

Suppose we have the graph of $f(x) = x^3 - x^2 - 2x + 1$.

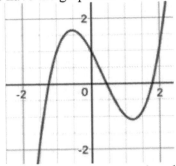

We want to find the zero of $f(x)$ between 0 and 1. I'll start Newton's Method with $x_0 = 1$.

What we're going to do first is find the tangent line of $f(x)$ at $x = 1$, and then find the x-intercept of that tangent line. We'll use point slope form with point $(1, -1)$.

$$f'(1) = -1 \quad y + 1 = -(x - 1) \implies y = -x$$

And the x-intercept is 0. Call this value x_1.

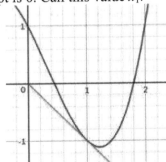

Then we find another tangent line and intercept for this new x value!

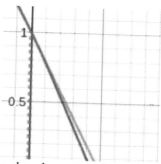

x_2 equals 0.5. We're already pretty close to the zero now, but let's just do one more iteration.

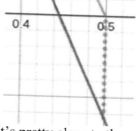

x_3 equals 0.4444. That's pretty close to the actual zero, which is 0.4450!

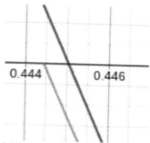

Generally, you should keep going until two successive x_n differ by less than 0.001.

As you can see, Newton's Method works by closing down on a point using the slope at specific points. You can get pretty accurate results with just a few iterations! Let's zoom out so you can see the big picture.

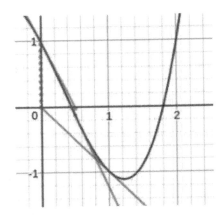

If you don't like remembering steps, there's a general formula for finding x_{n+1} given x_n and $f(x)$.

$$x_{n+1} = x_n - \frac{f(x_n)}{f'(x_n)}$$

But I'd suggest just remembering the steps, because it's more intuitive that way.

To save space, the following examples won't show much work when calculating x_n values.

EXAMPLE 3.8.1:

Given $f(x) = 1 - 2x^2$ and $x_0 = 1$, approximate the root of $f(x)$ to the nearest

You can calculate the x_n values with either method.

$$x_0 = 1$$
$$x_1 = 0.833$$
$$x_2 = 0.796$$
$$x_3 = 0.794$$
$$x_4 = 0.794$$

The root of the function is at x = 0.794.

You can also calculate specific values and intersections of two functions with Newton's Method.

$$f(x) = n \qquad\qquad f(x) = g(x)$$
$$f(x) - n = 0 \qquad\qquad f(x) - g(x) = 0$$
$$h(x) = f(x) - n \qquad h(x) = f(x) - g(x)$$

And now we can find the zero of $h(x)$ to locate the intersections.

EXAMPLE 3.8.2:

Approximate the intersections of $x - 2\sin(x)$ and $x^2 - 3$ to the nearest 0.001.

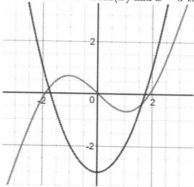

$$h(x) = x - 2\sin(x) - x^2 + 3 \implies h'(x) = 1 - 2\cos(x) - 2x$$

Let's use x = -2 and x = 2 as the starting values.

$$x_0 = 2.000 \qquad x_0 = -2.000$$
$$x_1 = 1.622 \qquad x_1 = -1.797$$
$$x_2 = 1.619 \qquad x_2 = -1.782$$
$$x_3 = 1.619 \qquad x_3 = -1.782$$

However, Newton's Method isn't foolproof. There are certain conditions in which Newton's Method fails, namely, if:
1. It hits a horizontal tangent. (The tangent line won't ever hit the *x*-axis.)
2. It goes back and forth between a few points. (The points won't converge to the root.)

EXAMPLE 3.8.3:

Approximate the root of $x^3 - 6x^2 + 10x - 6$ with $x_0 = 1$.

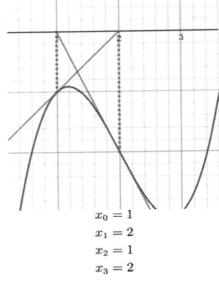

$$x_0 = 1$$
$$x_1 = 2$$
$$x_2 = 1$$
$$x_3 = 2$$
$$\vdots$$

Newton's Method goes back and forth between two values! It doesn't converge on the root of the function. We have to use a different initial value if we want to find the root.

3.9 - Differentials

A differential is just a small change in a value, denoted dx or dy or something of that form. Does this notation seem a bit familiar?

$$y = f(x) \implies \frac{dy}{dx} = f'(x) \implies dy = f'(x)dx$$

dy is just the change in y for a small change in x, or dx. We call dx the **differential of x** and dy the **differential of y**.

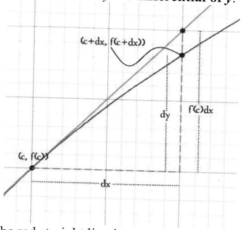

Notice that the red straight line is very close to the black function line at small values. In fact, we can use differentials to approximate values of functions, given that dx is small enough.

EXAMPLE 3.9.1:

Approximate the value of $\sqrt{16.2}$.

Let $y = \sqrt{x}$. Then $\dfrac{dy}{dx} = \dfrac{1}{2\sqrt{x}} \implies dy = \dfrac{1}{2\sqrt{x}}\,dx.$

Now we set $x = 16$ and $dx = 0.02$, because $x + dx = 16.2$.

$$dy = \frac{1}{2\sqrt{16}} \cdot 0.2 = 0.025$$

Since we know $y = \sqrt{x} = \sqrt{16} = 4$, $y + dy = \boxed{16.025}$.

$$\sqrt{16.2} = 16.0249.$$

Hey, pretty close to the actual value!

79

Differentials can be used to measure **propagated error** as well.
I'll explain through an example.

EXAMPLE 3.9.2:

A ball bearing is measured to be 0.14 inches in diameter, with an
error of $\pm$ 0.01 inches. Approximate the error in the volume.

Let's start by finding an equation relating diameter to volume.
$$V = \frac{4}{3}\pi r^3 = \frac{4}{3}\pi \left(\frac{d}{2}\right)^3 = \frac{4}{3}\pi \frac{d^3}{8} = \frac{1}{6}\pi d^3$$
Then we'll take the derivative.
$$V = \frac{1}{6}\pi d^3 \implies \frac{dV}{dd} = \frac{1}{2}\pi d^2$$
Finally, we'll multiply both sides by dd, the differential of d.
(Maybe I should have picked a different variable.)
$$dV = \frac{1}{2}\pi d^2 \cdot dd$$
But we know d and dd, because the problem gives us those
values! Let's plug them in.
$$dV = \frac{1}{2}\pi(0.14)^2 \cdot 0.01 \approx \boxed{0.000308 \text{ in}^3}$$

We can also compare this error to the calculated volume to get
the **percent error**.

EXAMPLE 3.9.3:

A ball bearing is measured to be 0.14 inches in diameter, with an
error of ± 0.01 inches. Approximate the percent error in the
volume.

It's the same problem as before, just with a different goal. I'll
pull dV down.
$$dV = 0.000308 \text{ in}^3$$
I'll also calculate the value of V with the diameter that's given.
$$V = \frac{1}{6}\pi(0.14 \text{ in})^3 \approx 0.00143$$
To find the percent error, we simply divide the propagated error
by the actual value.
$$\frac{dV}{V} = \frac{0.000308}{0.00143} \approx 0.214 = \boxed{21.4\%}$$

So what seems to be a small error actually turns out to be relatively large!

There are also problems that have you solve for original error, given propagated or percent error.

EXAMPLE 3.9.4:

A triangle has fixed side lengths of 3 and 4. The angle between those two sides is measured to be 60 degrees. Find the error in the measured angle if the percent error in the area of the triangle is 2%.

Let's first find an equation that relates angle to area.

$$A = \frac{1}{2}ab\sin(C) = \frac{1}{2}\cdot 3\cdot 4\cdot\sin(C) = 6\sin(C)$$

We know the sides 3 and 4 are fixed.

Next, we know the percent error, because the problem gives it to us.

$$\frac{dA}{A} = 0.02$$

We can calculate the equation for the differential of A.

$$A = 6\sin(C) \implies \frac{dA}{dC} = 6\cos(C) \implies dA = 6\cos(C)\cdot dC$$

$$A|_{C=90°} = 6\sin(90°) = 6$$

So, using the equation for the percent error:

$$\frac{dA}{A} = \frac{6\cos(C)\cdot dC}{6\sin(C)} = \cot(C)\cdot dC = 0.02$$

And using the angle given to us in the problem:

$$\cot(60°)\cdot dC = 0.02 \implies dC = 0.02\sqrt{3} \approx \boxed{0.035 \text{ radians}}$$

Remember, everything in calculus is based off radians! If the question specifically asked for the answer in degrees, <u>you can't write 0.035 degrees</u>! You have to convert it first.

$$0.035 \text{ radians} \approx \boxed{2.032°}$$

APPENDIX - COMMON DERIVATIVES AND RULES

Definition of the Derivative
$$f'(x) = \lim_{x \to \Delta x} \frac{f(x + \Delta x) - f(x)}{\Delta x}$$

Alternate Definition of the Derivative
$$f'(c) = \lim_{x \to c} \frac{f(x) - f(c)}{x - c}$$

Constant Rule (for any real number c)
$$\frac{d}{dx}c = 0$$

Constant Multiple Rule (for any real number c and differentiable function f)
$$\frac{d}{dx}c \cdot f(x) = c \cdot \frac{d}{dx}f(x)$$

Sum Rule (for differentiable functions f and g)
$$\frac{d}{dx}[f(x) + g(x)] = \frac{d}{dx}f(x) + \frac{d}{dx}g(x)$$

Power Rule (for any nonzero real number n)
$$\frac{d}{dx}x^n = nx^{n-1}$$

Product Rule (for differentiable functions f and g)
$$\frac{d}{dx}f(x)g(x) = f'(x)g(x) + f(x)g'(x)$$

Quotient Rule (for differentiable functions f and g)
$$\frac{d}{dx}\frac{f(x)}{g(x)} = \frac{f'(x)g(x) - f(x)g'(x)}{[g(x)]^2}$$

Chain Rule (for differentiable functions f and g)
$$\frac{d}{dx}f(g(x)) = f'(g(x))g'(x)$$

Trigonometric Derivatives

$$\frac{d}{dx}\sin(x) = \cos(x)$$

$$\frac{d}{dx}\cos(x) = -\sin(x)$$

$$\frac{d}{dx}\tan(x) = \sec^2(x)$$

$$\frac{d}{dx}\cot(x) = -\csc^2(x)$$

$$\frac{d}{dx}\sec(x) = \tan(x)\sec(x)$$

$$\frac{d}{dx}\csc(x) = -\cot(x)\csc(x)$$

Inverse Trigonometric Derivatives

$$\frac{d}{dx}\arcsin(x) = \frac{1}{\sqrt{1-x^2}}$$

$$\frac{d}{dx}\arccos(x) = -\frac{1}{\sqrt{1-x^2}}$$

$$\frac{d}{dx}\arctan(x) = \frac{1}{1+x^2}$$

$$\frac{d}{dx}\operatorname{arccot}(x) = -\frac{1}{1+x^2}$$

$$\frac{d}{dx}\operatorname{arcsec}(x) = \frac{1}{|x|\sqrt{x^2-1}}$$

$$\frac{d}{dx}\operatorname{arccsc}(x) = -\frac{1}{|x|\sqrt{x^2-1}}$$

Polar and Parametric Derivatives

$$\frac{dy}{dx} = \frac{\frac{dy}{dt}}{\frac{dx}{dt}}$$

$$\frac{dy}{dx} = \frac{\frac{dy}{d\theta}}{\frac{dx}{d\theta}}$$

$$\frac{d^2y}{dx^2} = \frac{\frac{d}{dt}\frac{dy}{dx}}{\frac{dx}{dt}}$$

Logarithmic Derivatives (for any positive a)

$$\frac{d}{dx}\ln(x) = \frac{1}{x}$$

$$\frac{d}{dx}\log_a(x) = \frac{1}{x\ln(a)}$$

Exponential Derivatives (for any positive a)

$$\frac{d}{dx}e^x = e^x$$

$$\frac{d}{dx}a^x = a^x\ln(a)$$

$$\frac{d}{dx}x^x = x^x(1+\ln(x))$$

Inverse Derivatives (for any differentiable function f)

$$\frac{d}{dx}f^{-1}(x) = \frac{1}{f'(f^{-1}(x))}$$

ACKNOWLEDGEMENTS

First of all, I'd like to thank Mrs. Moore, my calculus teacher, for teaching me everything I know about calculus. She's an amazing teacher and inspired me to publish this book in the first place. I'd also like to thank Mou Zhu, for helping me throughout the editing and publishing process. He's sacrificed a lot of his time helping me. I also want to mention my friends. They're the ones who I've written study guides for since 8th grade, and the ones I do all my work for. Finally, I want to thank my parents and my brother, who cheered me on through the entire process.

This book would not exist without any of you. Thank you all so much!